The
PUPPET
FACTORY

by Imogene Forte

Incentive Publications, Inc.
Nashville, Tennessee

Acknowledgements to:
Barbara Forte, cover and illustrations
Susan Oglander, editor

Library of Congress Catalog Number 83-82048

ISBN 0-86530-036-4

TABLE OF CONTENTS

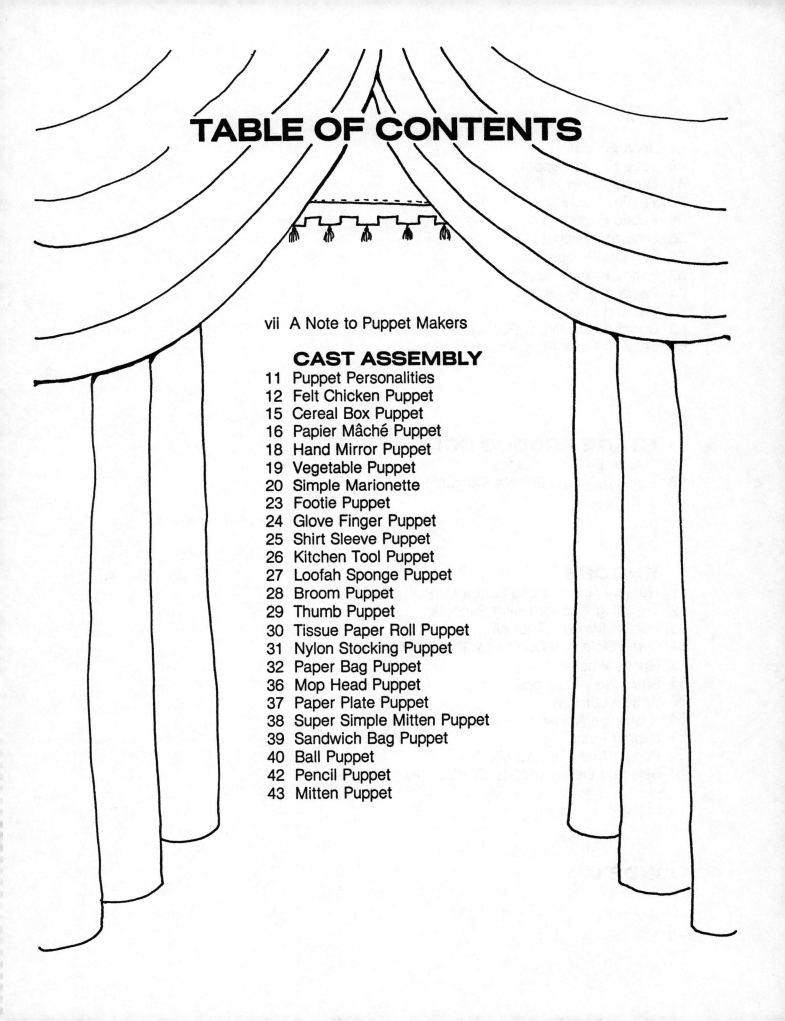

STAGE PRODUCTION

ENCORE

A NOTE TO PUPPET MAKERS

Here are some things you need to know before you begin to use this book.

. . . First, all of the puppets in this book are fun and easy to make. You can finish any or all of them without a lot of supplies, and you don't have to work long hours to have a finished product you can be proud of.

. . . Collect your materials so they are ready to use. You will need crayons, scissors, ruler, felt tip pens, construction paper, paints, paintbrush, glue or paste, pins, needle and thread, fabric scraps and yarn as basic supplies. Find a sturdy bag to hold your supplies. A paper shopping bag, last year's schoolbag, an old briefcase, a laundry bag or nylon net bag would work well. Once you have organized your supplies and added this book, your puppet factory will be ready for production.

. . . Go through the book to learn about the many kinds of puppets you can make and the creative ways they can be used. Then decide on the kind of puppet you want to make and how you want to use it. Perhaps it will be a puppet to use in a play with other puppets, to give as a gift or maybe you will want to make one just for fun!

. . . Always read the instructions completely, then gather your materials and arrange your work space before you start to work. It is also a good idea to check with the grownups to make sure that your plans meet with their approval.

. . . So select a puppet project that interests you, and get set to enjoy making and using puppets in some extraordinary ways.

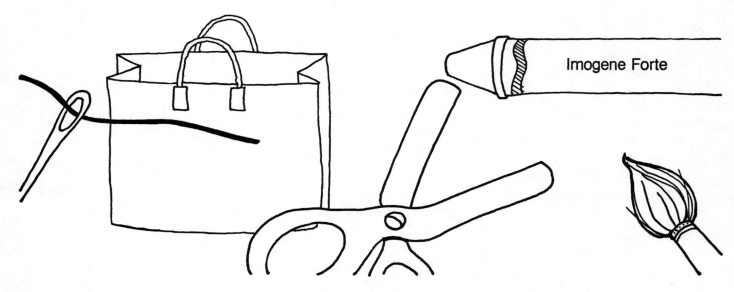

Imogene Forte

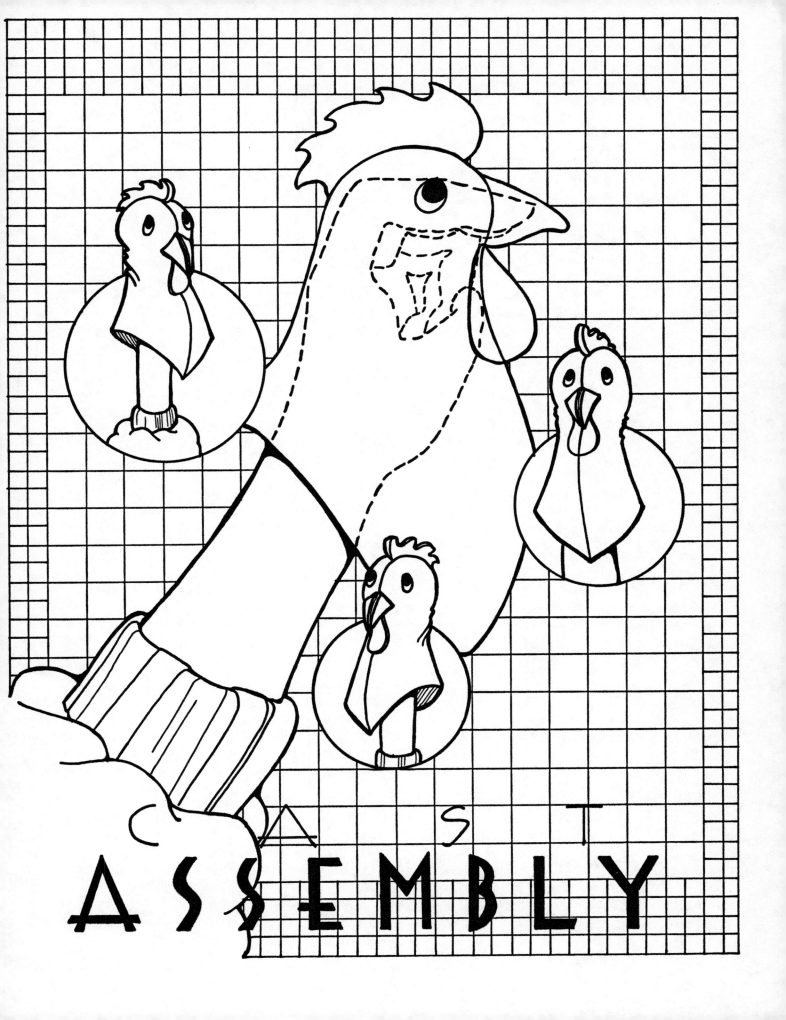

ASSEMBLY

PUPPET PERSONALITIES

All of the puppets in this book can be given faces and other interesting features from construction paper, felt, buttons, trim from the scrap box and felt tip pens.

These materials also can be used to give each puppet a personality and character all its own. Try making a puppet to show one of these traits.

sad
funny
silly
serious
happy
grateful
snobbish
boring
smart
peaceful
nervous
interesting
confused

clever
stupid
hungry
witty
humble
tricky
modern
surprised
old-fashioned
mysterious

FELT CHICKEN PUPPET

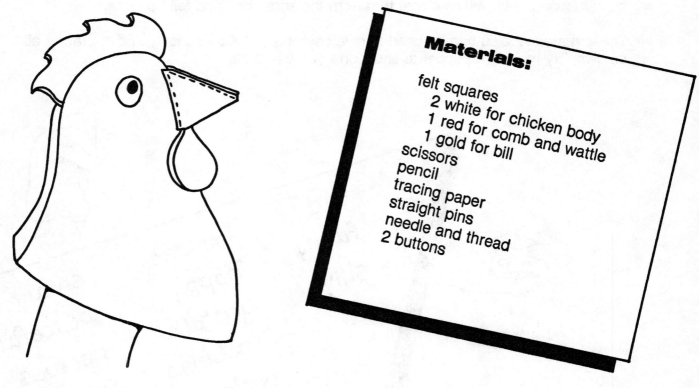

Materials:

felt squares
2 white for chicken body
1 red for comb and wattle
1 gold for bill
scissors
pencil
tracing paper
straight pins
needle and thread
2 buttons

Puppet Assembly:

1. Cut out the patterns on the following pages. 2. Pin on felt squares and cut out the shapes. 3. With right sides together, sew body pieces together as shown in figure A. (Be sure to leave enough open space at top to insert comb.) 4. Turn puppet body right side out. 5. Insert comb tab "a" (fig. B) and sew along seam line (fig. C). 6. With right sides together, sew bill as indicated in figure D. 7. Turn bill right side out and press seam flat. Press tabs "b" under, and stitch onto chicken face. 8. Stitch wattle under bill. 9. Sew on buttons for eyes where indicated on body pattern.

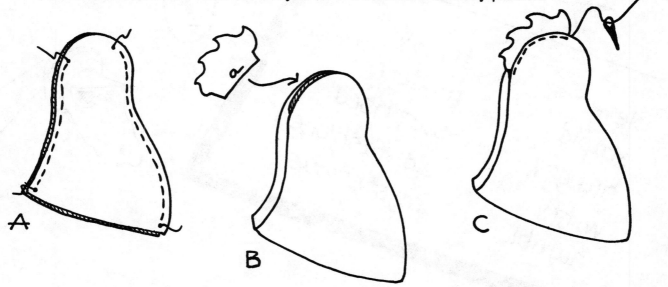

A

B

C

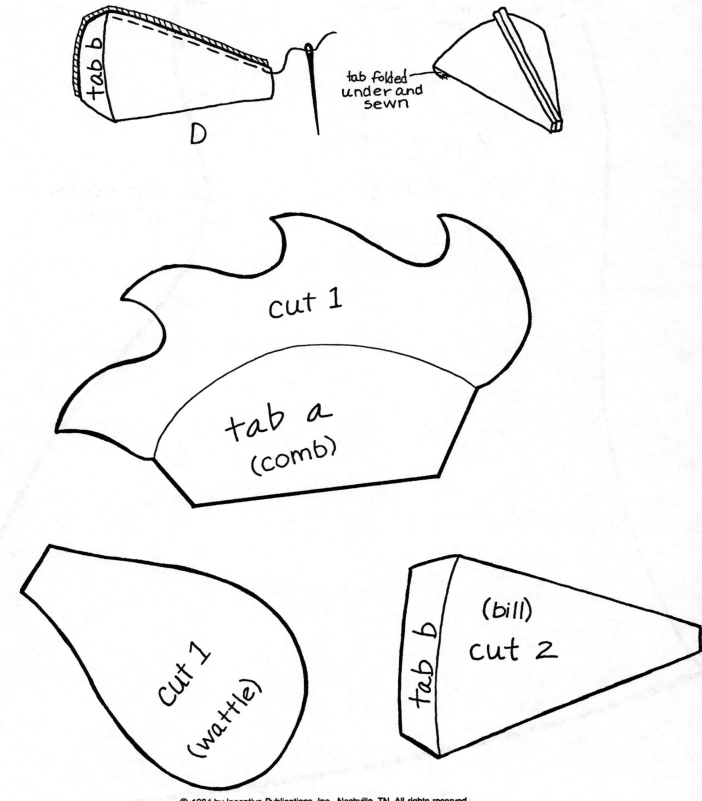

tab b

D

tab folded
under and
sewn

cut 1

tab a
(comb)

cut 1
(wattle)

(bill)
cut 2

tab b

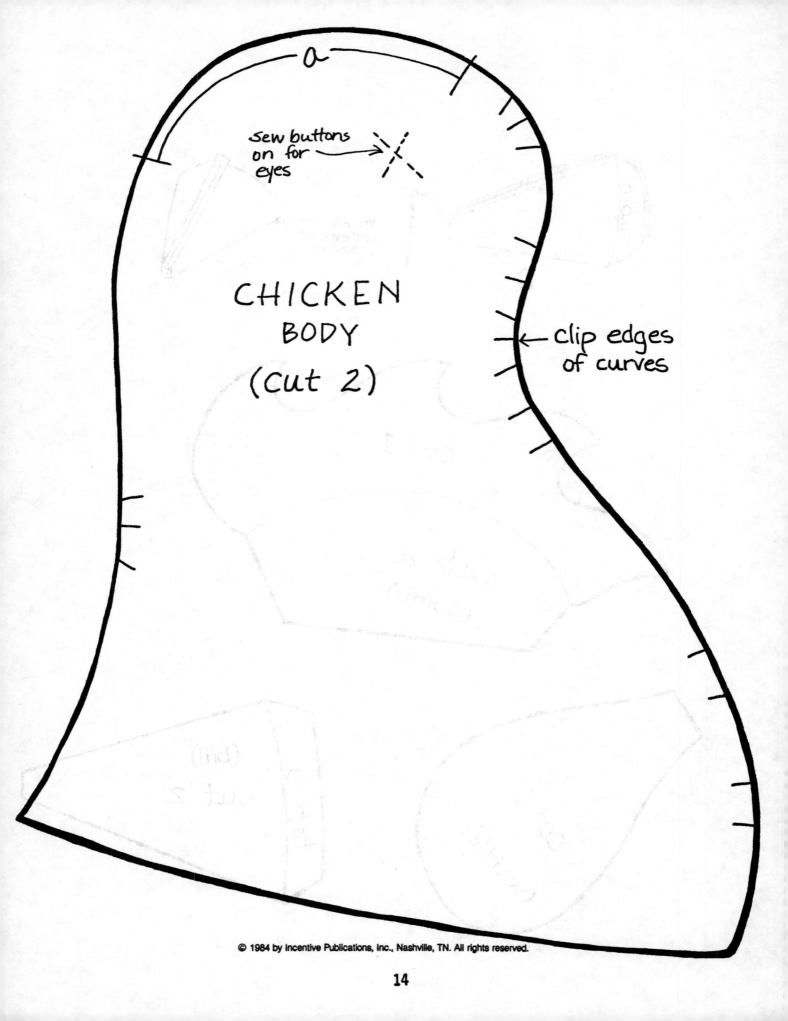

a

sew buttons on for eyes →

CHICKEN
BODY
(cut 2)

← clip edges of curves

CEREAL BOX PUPPET

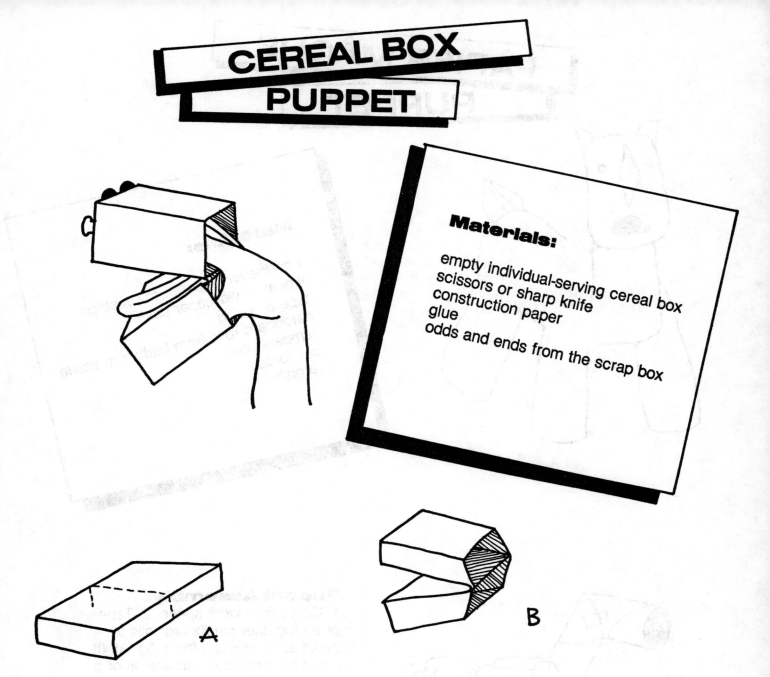

Materials:

empty individual-serving cereal box
scissors or sharp knife
construction paper
glue
odds and ends from the scrap box

A

B

Puppet Assembly:
1. Use the knife to cut 3 sides of the cereal box (fig. A). 2. Bend the sides back to fit your hand (fig. B). 3. Cover the cereal box with construction paper. Glue in place. 4. Decorate your cereal box puppet with odds and ends from the scrap box.

PAPIER MÂCHÉ PUPPET

Materials:

newspaper or paper towel strips
wheat or wallpaper paste
tape or string
cardboard rolls from bathroom tissue
tempera paint
paintbrush
varnish

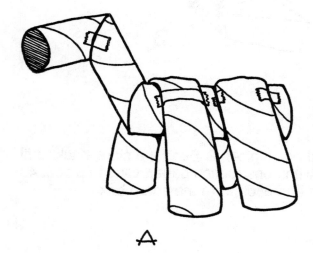

A

Puppet Assembly:

1. Cover your work space. 2. Tape or tie together cardboard rolls to make an interesting form (fig. A). (It could be a monster, an animal or a space creature.) 3. Mix the paste with cold water until it forms a creamy consistency. Make sure all the lumps are gone.

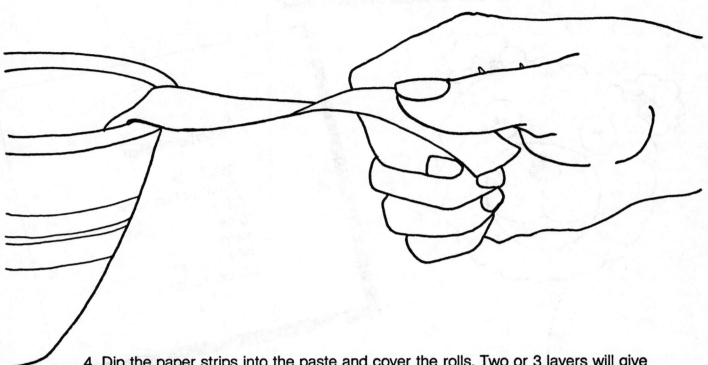

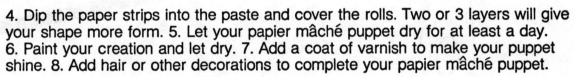

4. Dip the paper strips into the paste and cover the rolls. Two or 3 layers will give your shape more form. 5. Let your papier mâché puppet dry for at least a day. 6. Paint your creation and let dry. 7. Add a coat of varnish to make your puppet shine. 8. Add hair or other decorations to complete your papier mâché puppet.

TEMPERA
PAINT

HAND MIRROR PUPPET

Materials:

hand mirror
construction paper
felt
glue
yarn
fabric scraps
beads, buttons

Puppet Assembly:

1. Glue construction paper to the back of a hand mirror. 2. Decorate your puppet face with odds and ends to make it interesting.

Note
If you ask a friend to make a hand mirror puppet with you, you can turn your mirrors around so the audience can become characters in your play.

VEGETABLE
PUPPET

Materials:

green pepper
squash
carrot
onion
cloves, bell pepper strips,
carrot circles, raisins

Puppet Assembly:

1. Pick a vegetable you like and wash and dry it thoroughly. 2. Make a face for your puppet with carrot circles for eyes, a raisin for a nose, bell pepper strips for hair or whatever you like to make your vegetable puppet become an edible delight!

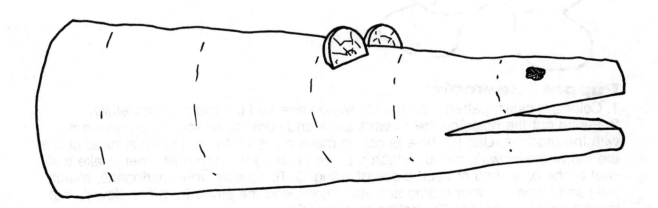

SIMPLE MARIONETTE

Materials:

crayons or felt tip pens
2 brads
string
scissors
hole punch (scissors will work)

Puppet Assembly:

1. Color the clown patterns on the following page and cut them out carefully.
2. Punch out the holes on the clown's arms and body. 3. Attach the clown's arms with the brads. 4. Use the hole punch to make holes at the end of each hand and at the top of the clown's hat. 5. Attach a piece of string to each hole. Then make a slip knot at the other end of each piece of string. 6. To operate your marionette, attach the hand strings to your thumb and little finger, and the string from the clown's hat to your index finger (see illustration on page 22).

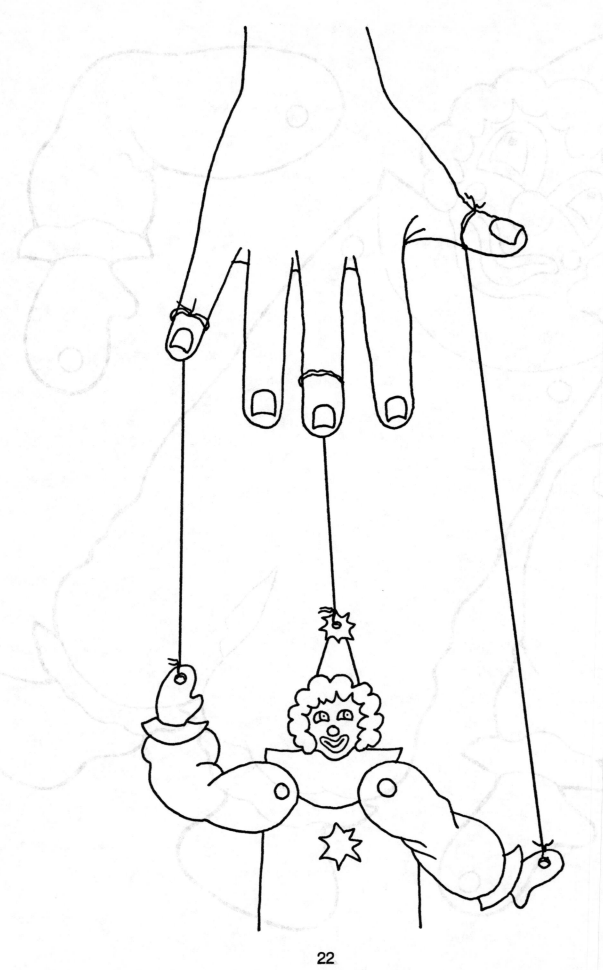

FOOTIE
PUPPET

Materials:

old footie
felt scraps
glue
buttons
needle and thread

Puppet Assembly:

1. Decorate the top or bottom of a footie with a face you like. 2. Place the footie over your hand and move your fingers to make different expressions.

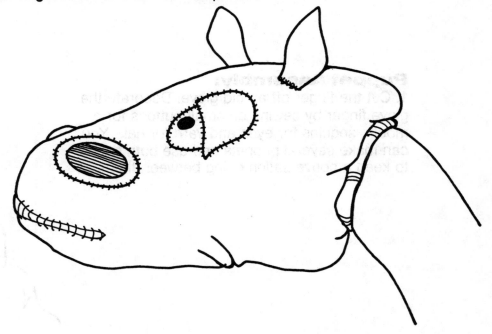

GLOVE FINGER PUPPET

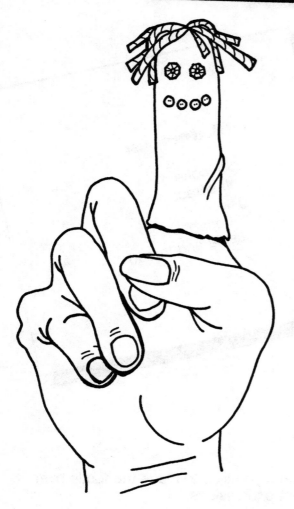

Materials:

old glove
scissors
sequins, yarn, small buttons
needle and thread

Puppet Assembly:

1. Cut the finger off an old glove. Decorate the glove finger by sewing on small buttons for a mouth, sequins for eyes and yarn for hair. You can make several puppets and use both hands to keep a conversation going between them.

SHIRT SLEEVE PUPPET

Materials:

old shirt sleeve
needle and thread
buttons
felt
scissors

Puppet Assembly:

1. Cut off an old shirt sleeve at the elbow. 2. Move the button on the cuff to make it fit your forearm right below your elbow, or remove the button and use 2 pieces of Velcro (fig. A). 3. Sew the cut end together with needle and thread. 4. Sew on buttons for eyes, a felt mouth, nose and ears.

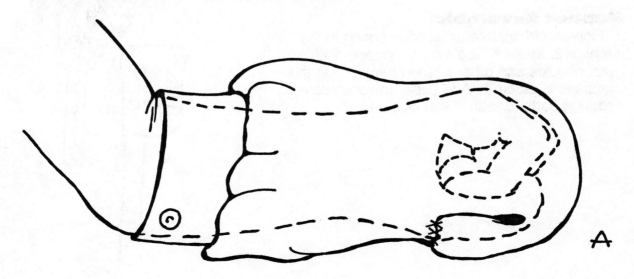

A

KITCHEN TOOL PUPPET

Materials:

spatula or wooden spoon
glue
nuts, noodles, seeds
paper towel strips or scouring pads

Puppet Assembly:

1. Find an old spatula or wooden spoon in the kitchen. 2. Make a face for your puppet with nuts, noodles and other kitchen items. Glue the materials in place. 3. Add paper towel strips or scouring pads for hair if you like.

LOOFAH SPONGE PUPPET

Materials:

loofah sponge (if you don't have one, a regular sponge will work)
odds and ends from the scrap box

Puppet Assembly:

1. Depending on the type of puppet you make, you can hold the sponge at the bottom with your hand, cut a space for your fingers, hide your hand under a handkerchief or stick a pencil in the sponge. 2. To give your puppet some real character, add a hat, sunglasses or a cigar!

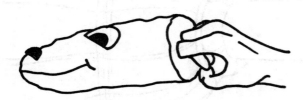

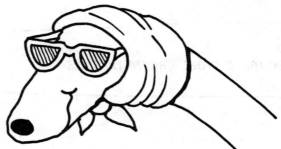

BROOM
PUPPET

Materials:

broom
old pillowcase
cloth strips
string
scissors
glue
felt tip pens or paints

Puppet Assembly:

1. Cover the broom bristles with the pillowcase. 2. Tie it in place with a piece of string. 3. Cut strips of cloth (an old sweater or pair of jeans would made great hair) and glue them in place. 4. Use the felt tip pens or paints to give your broom puppet an amusing face.

Note
These make great life-size puppets.

THUMB
PUPPET

Materials:

your thumb
washable felt tip pens

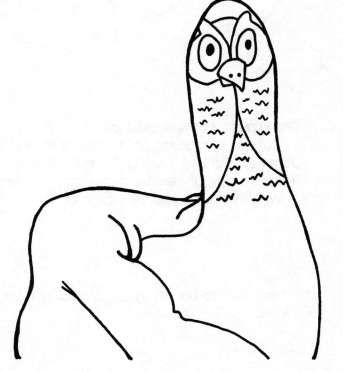

Puppet Assembly:

1. Make sure your thumb is clean.
2. Then, use the felt tip pens to make eyes, nose and a mouth. You can use both thumbs for more fun!

TISSUE PAPER ROLL PUPPET

Materials:

cardboard roll from bathroom tissue
construction paper
scissors
glue
felt tip pens

Puppet Assembly:

1. Cut the cardboard roll in half or long enough to fit 2 fingers. 2. Cut construction paper and glue it around the roll. 3. Draw the face of the character on the roll. 4. Add fringed strips of construction paper to make hair, paper hats, collars, neckties, skirts or whatever else you can think of.

Note
If you want to do a play all by yourself, you may want to make puppets for both hands.

NYLON STOCKING PUPPET

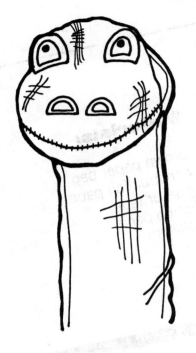

Materials:

nylon stockings
glue
odds and ends
scissors

Puppet Assembly:

1. Cut 1 nylon stocking so that it reaches your forearm when you put your hand inside. 2. Use the toe end of this stocking for your puppet. 3. Stuff the other stockings inside to give your puppet some shape. 4. Decorate your stocking puppet to suit your fancy. 5. Wiggle your hand in between the stockings to operate your puppet.

Note
These make great snake or dragon puppets.

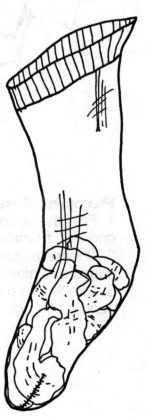

PAPER BAG PUPPET

Materials:

brown paper bag
construction paper
glue or tape
felt tip pens
scissors

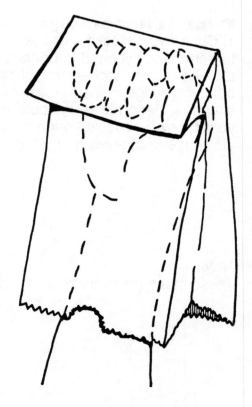

Puppet Assembly:

1. Fold the bottom of the bag flat against one side to make the space for your hand.
2. Choose patterns from the following 3 pages and glue or tape parts to paper bag.
3. Use felt tip pens to make your paper bag puppet colorful.

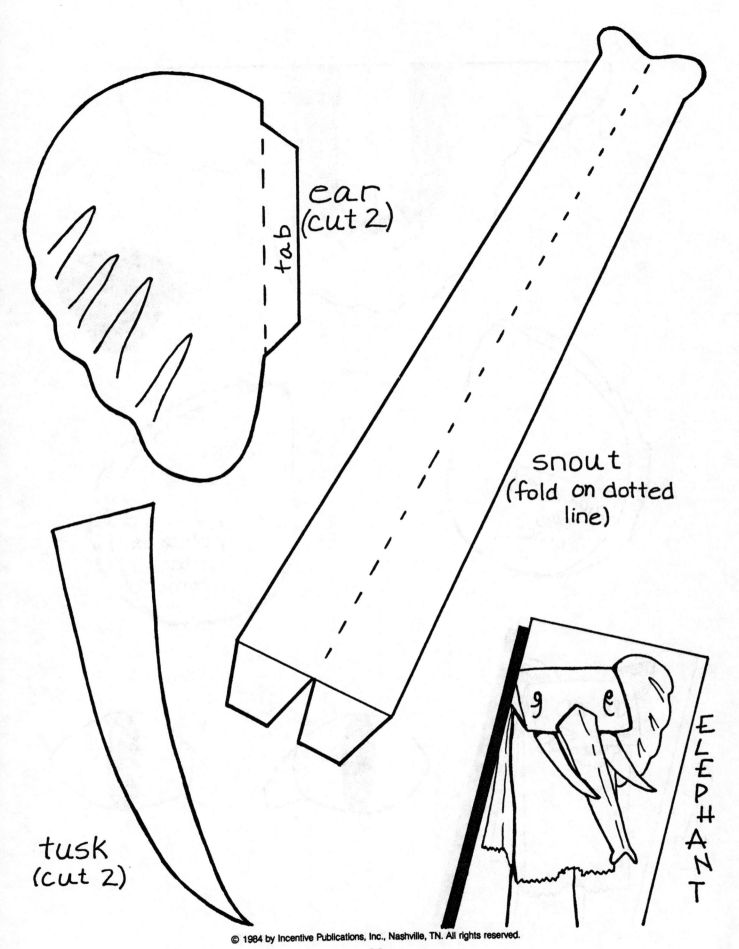

ear
(cut 2)

tab

snout
(fold on dotted
line)

tusk
(cut 2)

ELEPHANT

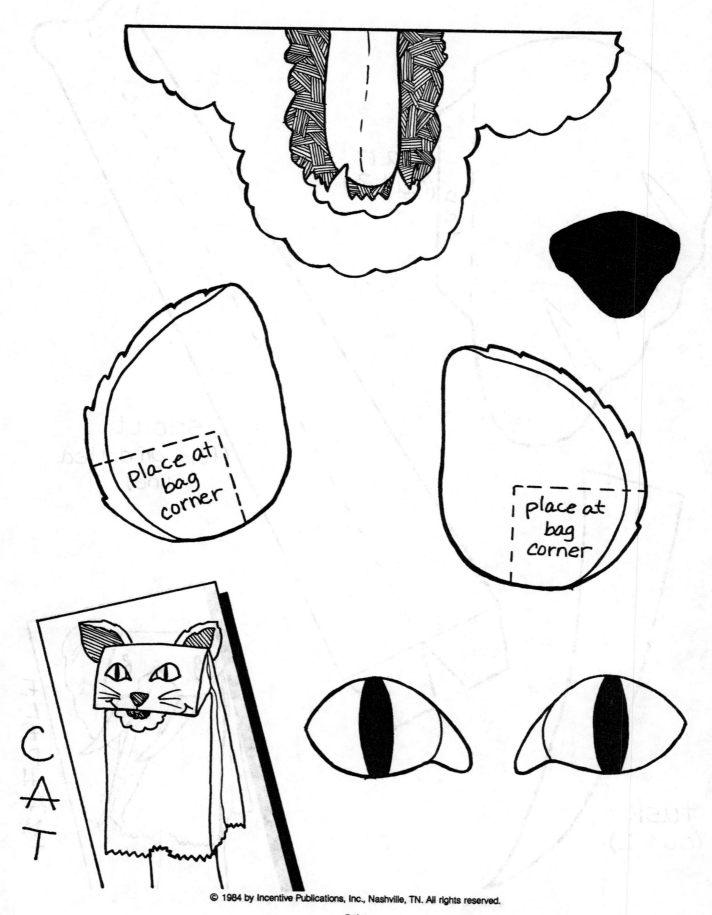

place at bag corner

place at bag corner

C
A
T

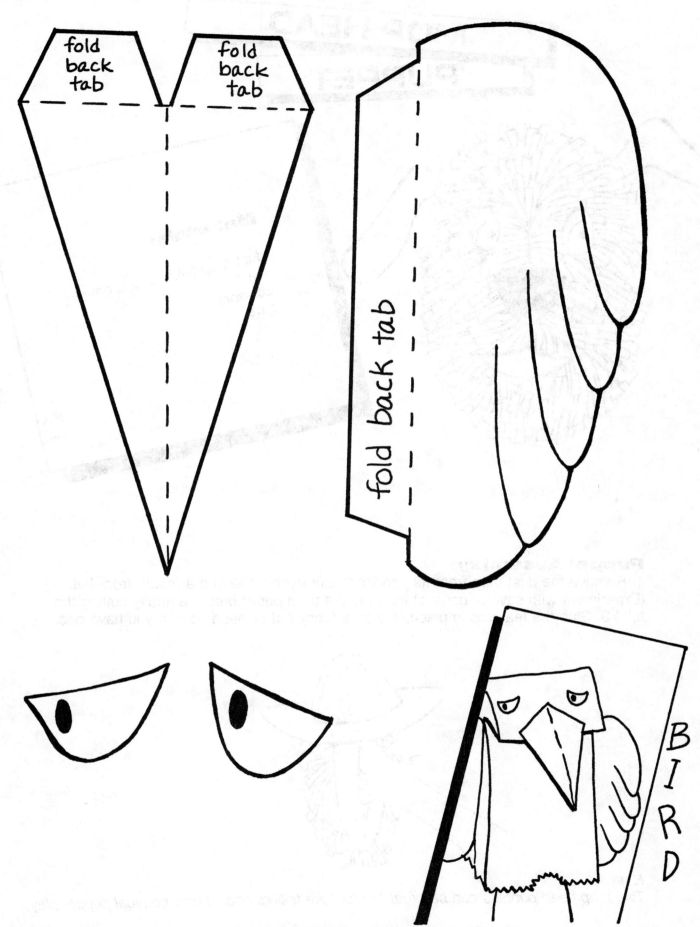

fold
back
tab

fold
back
tab

fold back tab

B I R D

MOP HEAD
PUPPET

Materials:

dust mop (without the handle)
felt
scissors
glue

Puppet Assembly:

1. Remove the dust mop from its handle. 2. Cut eyes, nose and a mouth from felt. (Experiment with several unusual features cut from paper before actually cutting the felt.) 3. Glue the features in place. 4. Add a funny hat or head scarf if you have one.

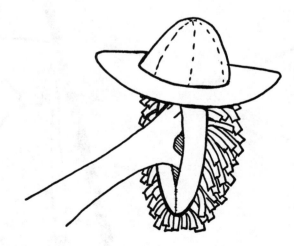

Note
Two mop head puppets can be great fun for joke telling, riddles or a comical puppet play.

PAPER PLATE PUPPET

Materials:

2 white paper plates
glue or stapler
crayons, felt tip pens, or paint
scissors
construction paper
odds and ends

Puppet Assembly:

1. Design the back of 1 plate with a creative face you like. Color, paint or draw eyes, nose and a mouth. 2. Cut another paper plate in half (fig. A). 3. Glue or staple it to the face-plate so that the inside of the plates are facing each other (fig. B). This is the space for your hand. 4. Finish your paper plate puppet with odds and ends from the scrap box, construction paper ears, a hat or earrings. You can make a small hole for the mouth, stick your finger out and wiggle it!

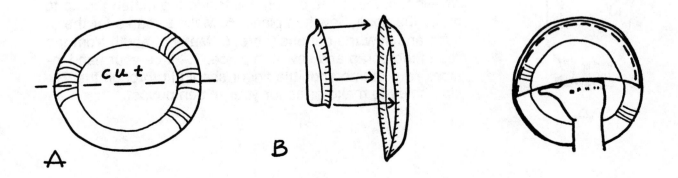

SUPER SIMPLE MITTEN PUPPET

Materials:

old mitten
needle and thread
glue
scissors
red fabric scrap
2 buttons
cotton ball

A

Puppet Assembly:

1. Cut the thumb off the mitten as shown in figure A. 2. Cut another hole approximately the same size on the opposite side. 3. Put a line of glue around the hole to help prevent raveling. 4. Place the cotton ball inside the mitten thumb to make the nose. Sew it in place. 5. Make 2 marks for the eyes and sew the buttons there. 6. Make a mouth from the red fabric scrap and sew it in place. 7. Place your hand inside. Your thumb and little finger should fit through the 2 side holes to make arms for your mitten puppet.

SANDWICH BAG PUPPET

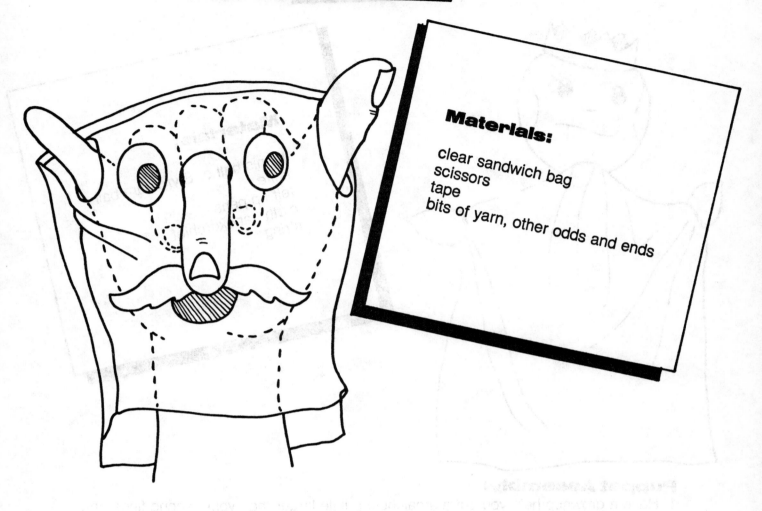

Materials:

clear sandwich bag
scissors
tape
bits of yarn, other odds and ends

Puppet Assembly:

1. Cut 2 holes in the sides of the sandwich bag big enough for your thumb and little finger. These will be the puppet's arms. 2. Cut another hole for the nose. Put your middle finger through this hole. 3. Decorate your puppet by taping on bits of yarn or other odds and ends.

BALL
PUPPET

Materials:

tennis ball or Styrofoam ball
knife
felt tip pens
cloth handkerchief
string

Puppet Assembly:

1. Have a grownup help you cut a small hole a little larger than your second finger in the ball. 2. Use felt tip pens to make a face on the ball. Add hair, ears or a crown if you want. 3. For the puppet's body, drape the handkerchief over your hand. Then push your finger into the hole in the ball. Use your little finger and your thumb for the puppet's arms. To help define the ball puppet's arms, tie a loose piece of string around each finger.

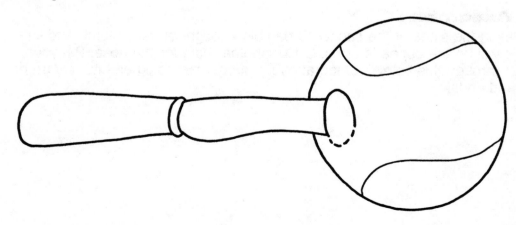

PENCIL
PUPPET

Materials:

pencil
cotton or tissues
yarn
tissue paper, white cloth or handkerchief
felt tip pens

Puppet Assembly:

1. Wrap some cotton or paper tissues around the top of the pencil. 2. Cover the padded pencil top with tissue paper, white cloth or a handkerchief. 3. Tie the covering tightly with yarn to form a "neck." 4. Use felt tip pens to make eyes, nose and mouth. 5. Add yarn or string hair, buttons and bows or any other decorations you like to give personality to your pencil puppet.

MITTEN
PUPPET

Materials:

mitten
2 buttons
straight pins
felt
needle and thread

Puppet Assembly:
1. Put the mitten on your hand and mark places for the eyes, nose and ears. 2. Cut 2 ears and a nose out of felt. 3. Sew the buttons in place for the eyes and then sew the ears and nose on your mitten puppet.

Note
Practice moving your fingers to make your mitten puppet come alive.

ear
(cut 2)

SOCK PUPPET

Materials:

old sock
felt tip pens
scissors
glue
posterboard
pencil

Puppet Assembly:

1. Trace an oval around your hand as you place it palm down on a piece of posterboard (fig. A). Cut the oval out. 2. Fold it in half (fig. B) and place glue on both inside flaps. 3. Turn your sock inside out and slip your hand inside so your fingers are in the toe and the heel is over your wrist.

A

B

glue

4. Place your hand in between the glued sides of the oval (fig. C). 5. Have a friend pull the sock off your arm and over the top of the oval, turning the sock right side out. 6. Give your sock puppet some personality by adding hair, horns, eyes, a hat or whatever else your imagination allows. 7. Place your hand inside and move your fingers and thumb to operate your sock puppet's mouth.

C

TUBE FINGER PUPPET

Materials:

white paper
tape
felt tip pens
colored paper, yarn

Puppet assembly:

1. Cut a strip of paper to fit around your finger (or as many fingers as you want to make puppets for).
2. Wrap the paper around your finger to make a tube (fig. A). 3. Decide what character you want to make and use the felt tip pens to draw its face. Use colored paper and any other trim you have to make hats, ties, earrings, clothes or other interesting add-ons.

A

4. When the tube is fully decorated, use tape to fasten it together (fig. B).

B

NURSERY RHYME PUPPET

Materials:

scissors
felt tip pens
glue
posterboard

Puppet Assembly:

1. Color the finger puppets on the following pages with felt tip pens. 2. Glue the colored puppets to a sheet of posterboard the same size and shape as the puppet. 3. Cut around the dotted lines for each puppet, then cut out the holes in each puppet. (Ask an adult for help if you need it.) 4. Stick your fingers through the holes to make legs for your nursery rhyme puppet.

Hansel
and
Gretel

Three Billy Goats Gruff

Little Red
Riding
Hood

51

WHOLE HAND PUPPET

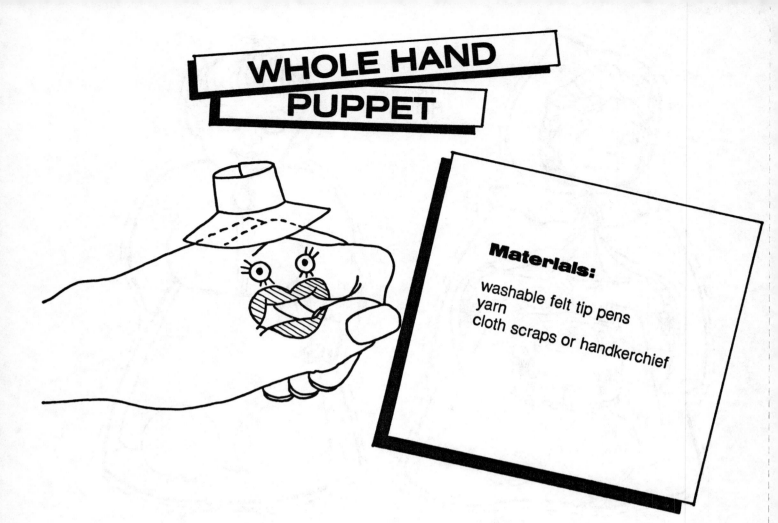

Materials:

washable felt tip pens
yarn
cloth scraps or handkerchief

Puppet Assembly:

1. Place your hand as shown in figure A. 2. Look at your hand and decide what kind of puppet character you want to create. To help you make this decision you can move your thumb around to get the feel of a mouth opening and closing. You can also practice making the mouth talk, cough, laugh and sing. Then try wiggling the whole hand and the thumb at the same time. 3. Use the pens to draw lips, eyes and a nose (or use mom's old makeup). Add a mustache, beard, dimples, or freckles for interest. 4. If you want to get fancy, you can use yarn or cloth to add a hat, hair, scarf or ears.

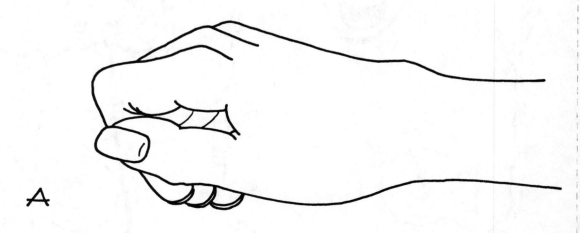

A

FABRIC
PUPPET

Materials:

½ yard of colorful fabric
tracing paper
pencil
scissors
straight pins
needle and thread

Puppet Assembly:

1. Cut out the patterns on the following pages. 2. Fold the fabric in half as shown in figure A. 3. Pin the front pattern along fold line as shown in figure B. Pin back pattern alongside front pattern as shown in figure B. 4. Carefully cut out patterns along solid black lines. (Do not cut along fold line on front pattern.) You will have 2 back pieces and 1 front piece. 5. Pin right sides of the backs together and stitch along dotted line as shown on pattern piece (fig. C).

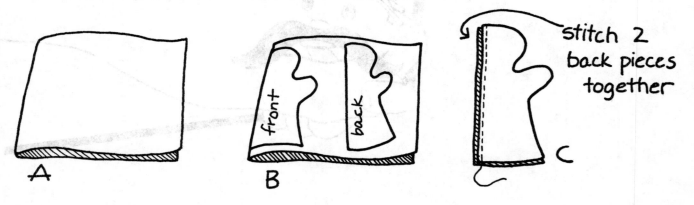

stitch 2 back pieces together

A   B   C

6. Place right sides of front and back together and stitch along dotted line (fig. D).
7. Turn puppet right side out and press. 8. You may need to hem the bottom of the puppet—if so, turn fabric ¼ inch to the inside and stitch. 9. Decorate your fabric puppet with beads, buttons, yarn, shells, nuts and whatever other odds and ends you can find.

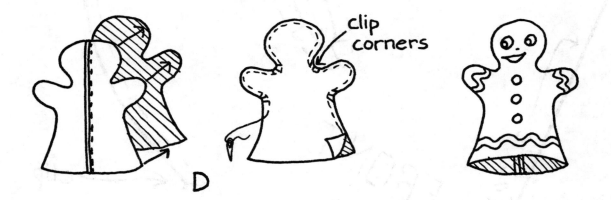

D

clip corners

This is a good pattern for a Christmas angel or any other winged creature.

wing
(cut 2)

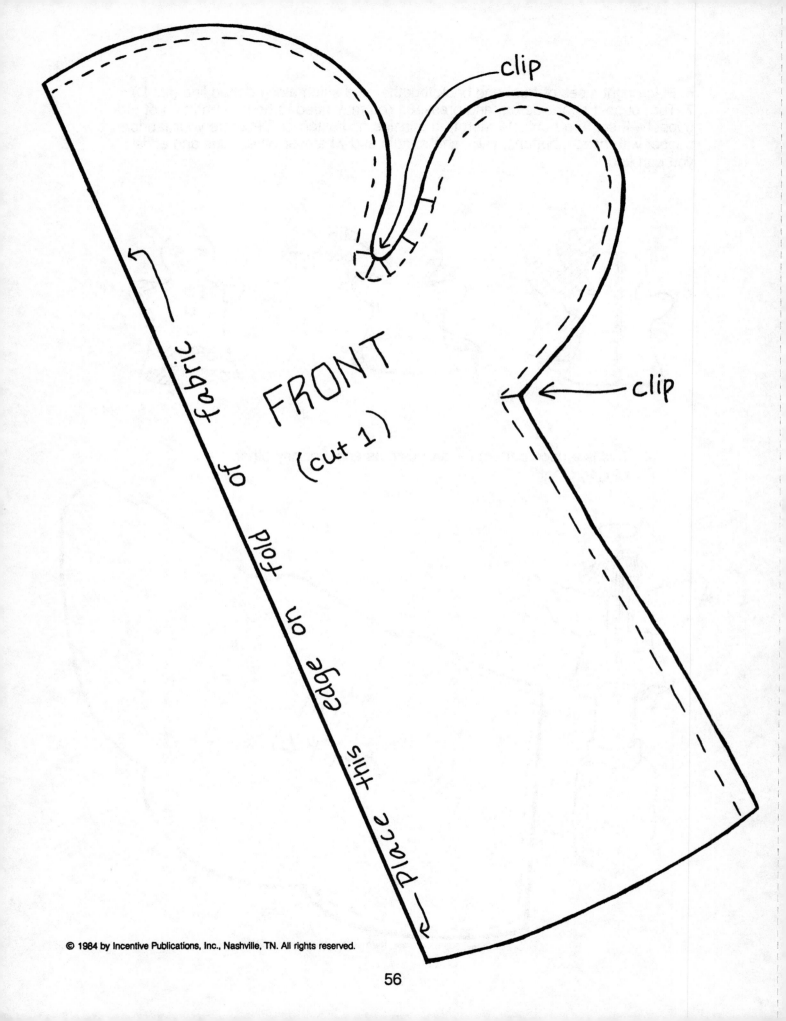

clip

clip

FRONT
(cut 1)

Place this edge on fold of fabric

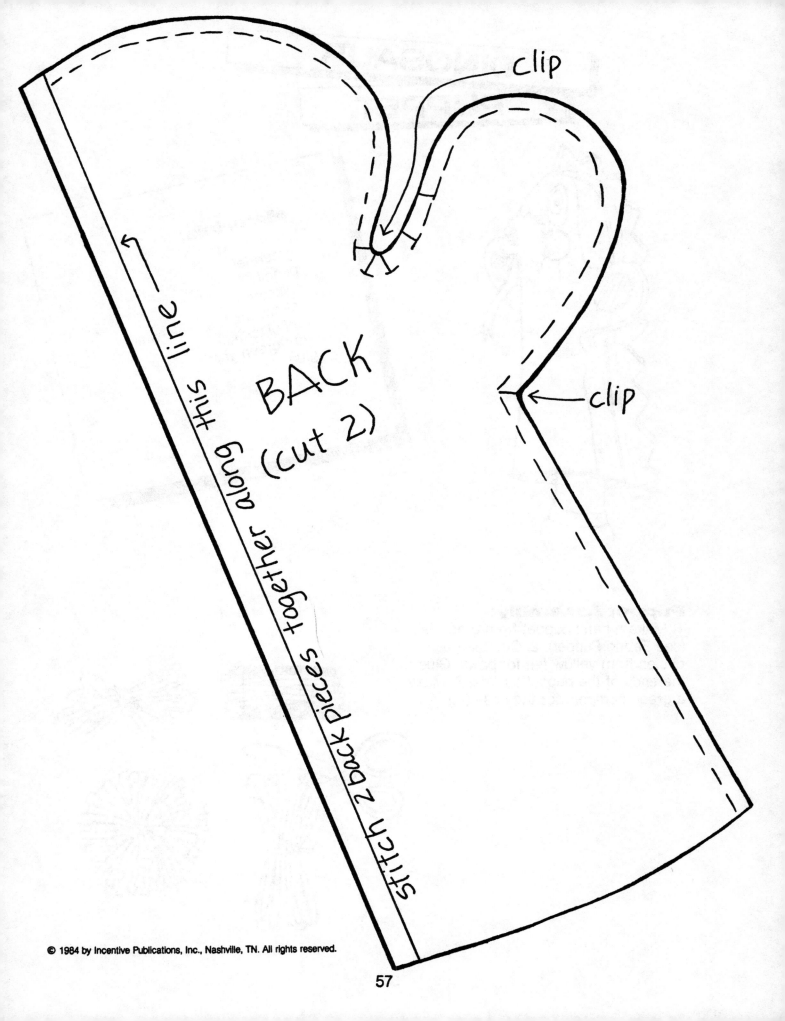

clip

BACK
(cut 2)

clip

stitch 2 back pieces together along this line

DINOSAUR
PUPPET

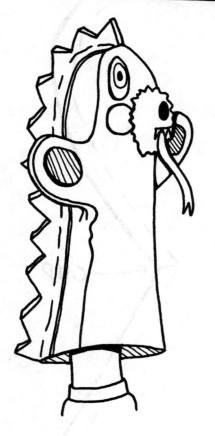

Materials:

green felt
pencil
scissors
yellow, orange, pink, white
and black felt
light green yarn
glue

Puppet Assembly:

1. Make a hand puppet from green felt (see Fabric Puppet). 2. Cut 2 large circles from yellow felt for paws. Glue to the ends of the puppet's arms. 3. Make a green pompom for the nose (fig. A).

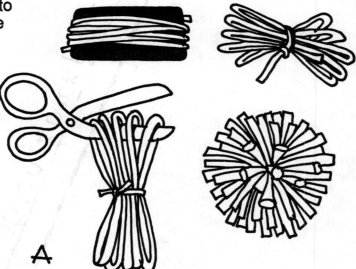

A

B

4. Glue a black circle to the end of the pompom. 5. Cut 2 to 4 teeth from white felt and glue these to the pompom.
6. Cut a pink tongue from the felt and glue it to the pompom (fig. B).

7. To make the dinosaur's eyes, cut 2 ovals from yellow felt, 2 eyes from orange felt and 2 small pupils from black felt. Glue the pieces together as shown in figure C.

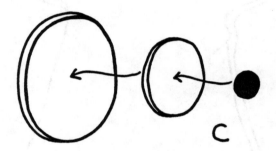

C

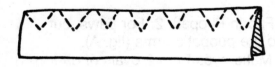

D

8. Cut 2 large circles of orange felt for cheeks. 9. To make your dinosaur's scales, cut a strip of orange triangles and glue it to the puppet's back (fig. D).

FELT LION PUPPET

Materials:

yellow or gold felt
pencil
scissors
glue
orange, pink, dark green
and dark yellow felt
yellow yarn

Puppet Assembly:

1. Make a hand puppet from yellow or gold felt (see Fabric Puppet). 2. For paws, cut 2 large orange circles and 6 small circles and glue to the puppet's arms (fig. A).
3. Make a nose from a triangle of pink felt (fig. B). 4. Make eyes from 2 ovals of dark green felt and 2 circles of dark yellow felt. Glue the circles on the 2 ovals (fig. C).

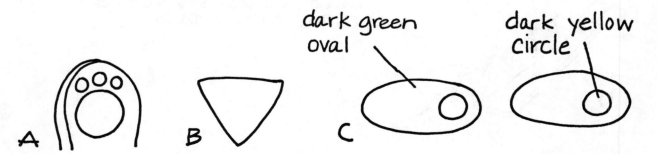

dark green oval

dark yellow circle

A   B   C

5. Make the lion's mane by cutting a large circle of dark yellow felt and a smaller circle of orange felt (fig. D). Be sure to fringe the ends of the mane. Glue the center of the small mane to the back of the puppet's head. Then glue the center of the large mane to the center of the small mane. 6. Finish your felt lion puppet by making 2 pompoms from yellow yarn and placing them under his nose (see page 58).

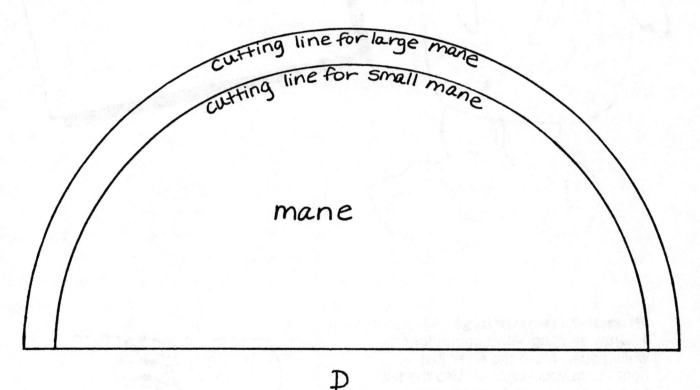

D

FANCY FINGER PUPPET

Materials:

white paper
felt tip pens
tape
pencil

Puppet Assembly:

1. Draw an imaginative character on white paper. Make the size "just right" to fit your finger. 2. Use the felt tip pens to color and add interest to the puppet.

A

B

3. Cut out a strip of paper to go around your finger. Glue it to the character (fig. A). 4. Add a piece of tape to fasten the puppet around your finger (fig. B).

PAPER CUP
PUPPET

Materials:

paper cup
pencil
construction paper
felt tip pens
glue
buttons, sequins

Puppet Assembly:

1. Use a pencil to punch 2 holes in the bottom of the cup. (The holes are for your fingers.) 2. Draw facial features on the cup using the patterns and ideas on the following page. Use felt tip pens or construction paper to complete the face and make a hat, hair or add other finishing touches. 3. Buttons, trim or other stuff from your "good junk collection" can be used to add extra interest.

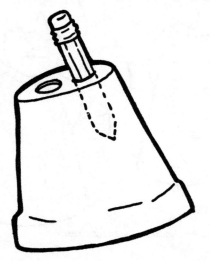

marker

PARTS DEPT.

WALKING
PUPPET

Materials:

characters from magazines, old storybooks or comics
scissors
glue
cardboard

Puppet Assembly:

1. Find the character you want for your puppet and cut it out. 2. Cut a piece of cardboard a little longer than the character you have chosen. 3. Fold the cardboard twice, once about 1 inch from the bottom edge, and again about 1½ inches from the bottom edge (figures A through C).

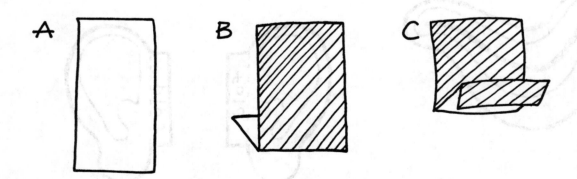

A

B

C

D

4. Cut 2 holes in the bottom fold (fig. D). 5. Glue the character onto the cardboard so that its knees fall just above the fold, its feet and legs under the fold. 6. Cut around the character. 7. Stick your fingers through the 2 holes to make the puppet walk, run, jump or dance.

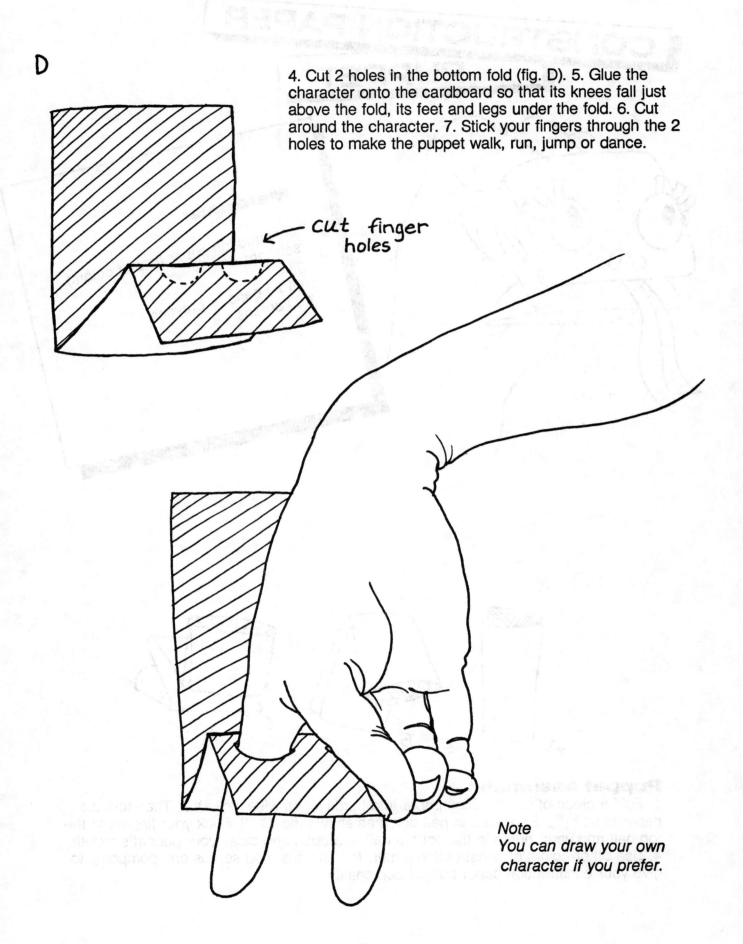

cut finger holes

Note
You can draw your own character if you prefer.

CONSTRUCTION PAPER PUPPET

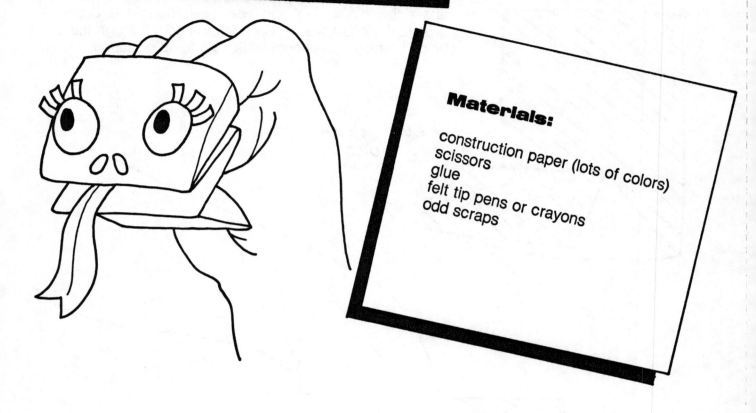

Materials:

construction paper (lots of colors)
scissors
glue
felt tip pens or crayons
odd scraps

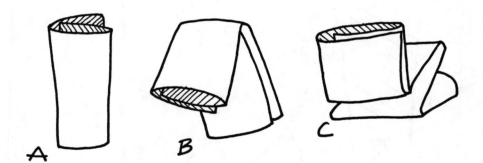

A   B   C

Puppet Assembly:

1. Fold a piece of construction paper into thirds lengthwise (fig. A). 2. Then fold the paper in half (fig. B). Fold it in half again as shown (fig. C). 3. Stick your fingers in the top half and your thumb in the bottom half and open and close your puppet's mouth. 4. Use other colors of construction paper, felt tip pens, odd scraps and pompoms to give your construction paper puppet personality.

EASY-TO-MAKE PUPPETS

Here are some basic, easy-to-make puppets that can be used over and over by kids who love to act out stories, real-life situations, puppet plays or lots of just-for-fun activities.

paper cup puppets

sock puppets

mitten puppets

paper bag puppets

paper plate puppets

simple cloth hand puppets

finger puppets

cereal box or milk carton puppets

STAGE
PRODUCTION

Any puppet play is more interesting when you use your imagination and surprise your audience by presenting your play from an original "made by you" stage.

Clever stages are not as hard to make as you may think. As a matter of fact, you may look around to find some "ready to use" stages just waiting to become part of a puppet play.

Have you thought about using . . .

- a table turned on its side—you stay on one side, your audience on the other side, and the puppets perform on the top edge.

- a card table with a sheet or blanket draped over it—you work from behind the table and use the tabletop as your stage.

- an overturned chair—this will work if you need a stage in a hurry and there is nothing else around. Drape a coat or shawl over the chair and kneel down in back of it.

• a tablecloth tacked or taped across a doorway—ask your audience to sit on the opposite side of the door as you hide behind the tablecloth and hold your puppets above the cloth.

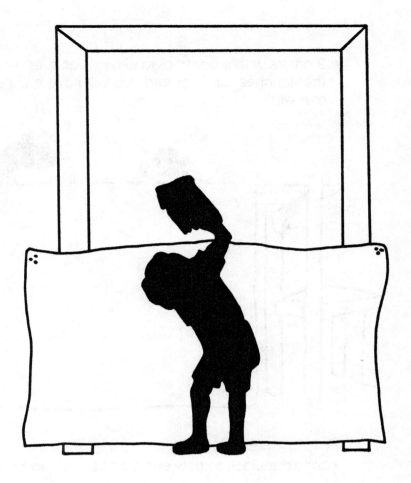

• a windowsill where the audience can sit on one side of the window and you on the other—this works especially well if you have a window shade that can be raised or lowered to give you a "stage curtain."

- 2 chairs with a board placed between them—cover the board with an old sheet that touches the floor and you will have a super stage from which several people can work.

- an old tablecloth between 2 trees—for an outside stage.

- a low bush—kneel behind it and use the top of the bush for the stage.

- an upturned shoe box with 1 side cut out—this makes a great stage for finger puppets.

shoe box

- a shallow box top with 2 holes cut for your hands to fit through—this will make a fine stage for a "traveling" puppet show. Just fasten sturdy string to the 4 corners so that the box top will hang from your neck. Stick your hands through the holes, put the puppets on your hands and on with the show! This is a good way to use a puppet show for party entertainment or to announce special events in classrooms or to family members.

- 3 sides of a refrigerator box (set up vertically)—with a rectangle cut out for the stage.

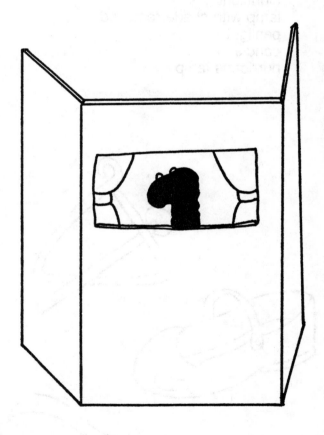

LIGHTING, SOUND EFFECTS, COSTUMES

The right lighting, sound effects and costumes can be a real help in making your puppet play believable. Here are some suggestions for simple ways to make your play come alive:

Lighting
flashlight
nightlight
lamp with shade removed
penlight
candle
hurricane lamp

Sound Effects
musical instruments being played
shoes striking a hard surface
clapping of hands
a book being closed firmly
a fingernail rasping against sandpaper
rocks stirred in aluminum pie pan
a whistle being blown

All the above sounds can be recorded and played for a special puppet play!

Costumes
construction paper
old doll clothes
cut up pillowcases colored with felt tip pens
glasses/sunglasses
hats
corduroy pant leg stuffed with paper
net
pipe
dishcloths
bandanna
old jewelry

ENCORE

Song/Rhyme	Puppet Characters	Props
Little Boy Blue	Little Boy Blue, sheep, cow	horn, haystack, corn-stalks
A Frog Went A Courting	Frog, Uncle Rat, Miss Mouse, Tom Cat, Bumble Bee, Miss Flea, Mistress Rat	food, drinks, saddle and bridle
Old King Cole	Old King Cole, Three Fiddlers	pipe, bowl, fiddles
Little Bo-Peep	Little Bo-Peep, sheep	crook, sheep's tails, handkerchief
Frère Jacques	Brother John, bell ringer	bed, bell
Rock-A-Bye, Baby	baby	tree, cradle
Jingle Bells	children, horse	sleigh, bells
Round The Mulberry Bush	boys and girls	none (actions can be carried out without props)
Oats, Peas, Beans, And Barley Grow	farmer, wife	none
The Farmer In The Dell	farmer, wife, child, nurse, dog, cat, rat, cheese	none
A Tisket, A Tasket	girl, little boy	basket, letter
Round The Village	boy, girl	house with windows big enough for puppets to go through (could be made from shoe box)
The Eency Weency Spider	spider, sun	water spout, something to make the sound of rain

TEACHING TIPS FOR USING PUPPETS

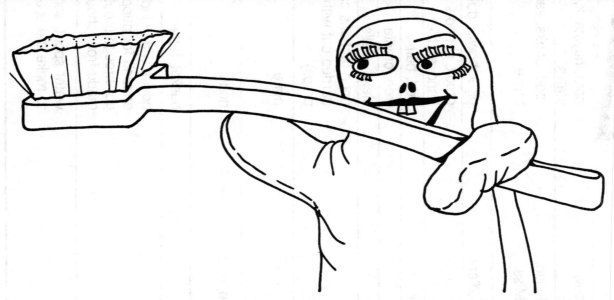

Puppets can be used in the classroom to teach, reteach, drill, motivate, introduce new concepts or just to entertain.

Maybe some of these teaching tips will serve as springboards for your own list.

Use a puppet or puppets to:

- Introduce a new child to the group and tell some special things about him or her to encourage the other children to want to get acquainted.

- Present dental health tips to the group—use questions asked by the puppet and answered by the children. Demonstrate proper brushing and flossing.

- Tell stories in the first person (the main character "doing the talking").

- Lead group singing.

- Lead a spelling bee.

- Introduce children to various handicaps that cannot be explained easily with real people (blindness, deafness, cerebral palsy).

- Help build an awareness of other cultures. (Each child could make a puppet representing a different country.)

- Reinforce self-concept. Children could make a puppet of themselves and act out various feelings, attitudes and opinions about important issues.

- Explore the career world. Puppets could role play employer and employee and practice interviewing and filling out an application.

PUPPET MAKER'S TOOL KIT

Begin to collect the things you will need to make puppets.

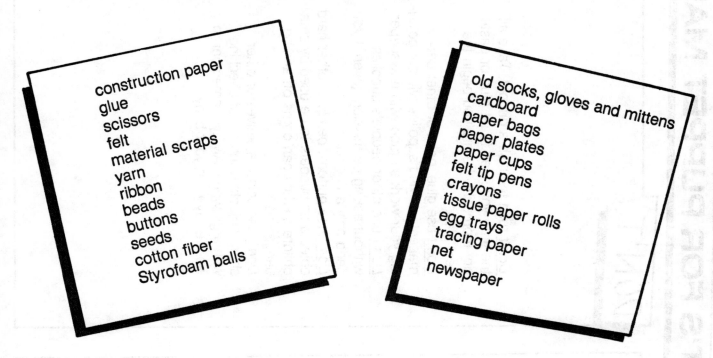

construction paper
glue
scissors
felt
material scraps
yarn
ribbon
beads
buttons
seeds
cotton fiber
Styrofoam balls

old socks, gloves and mittens
cardboard
paper bags
paper plates
paper cups
felt tip pens
crayons
tissue paper rolls
egg trays
tracing paper
net
newspaper

You can make heads for hand puppets from any number of things.

Try some of these and then use your imagination to find some others.

Styrofoam eggs
burned out lightbulbs
dish scrubbers
potatoes
apples

modeling clay
play dough
old stuffed animal heads
doll heads
balls of yarn

SOME DO'S AND DON'T'S FOR PUPPET MAKERS

DO

Do keep your work space neat and orderly when working.

Do always clean up and put your supplies away when finished.

Do gather all the needed supplies and equipment *before* you begin work.

Do think about the puppet you want to make before you begin working. If you are using written directions or suggestions, read them all the way through very carefully. If you are making a creative puppet from your own idea, make a sketch to work from.

Do read directions on glue, paint and other containers, and follow all the safety instructions.

Do try to add your own creative touch to every puppet you make so that it will be truly "yours."

DON'T

Don't rush to finish a puppet. Take all the time you need to let glue or paste dry thoroughly before you begin the next step.

Don't use glue, paint or other permanently drying supplies without covering your work surface with newspaper.

Don't use other people's supplies without asking permission, (even if you need only a tiny bit).

Don't use buttons, beads or other hard objects on puppets to be used by small children. (They can come off and be dangerous.)

Don't use scissors, knives or other sharp objects without first checking with a grownup. Always remember to work away from your body.

GUESS WHO?

Interview a classmate you find interesting. Note some important facts about the person.

Full name _____

Height_____ Weight_____ Color of hair_____

Date and place of birth _____

Number and ages of brothers and sisters _____
_____

Favorite things (sport, school subject, movie, TV show, hero) _____
_____
_____

Special talents _____
_____

Ambition or special wish _____
_____
_____

Now use the information you have gathered to prepare a lively and entertaining puppet script to present to the class. Let the puppet present one fact at a time until someone guesses the person being described.

SHOW HOW IT'S DONE

Use the finger puppets below to help demonstrate how to do one of the following things:
1. Wrap a package and tie it with a ribbon bow.
2. Peel an apple and take the core out.
3. Make a paper airplane and fly it.
4. Build a rope swing and tie it from a tree branch.

Color and cut out the puppets. Use one on each hand (sticking your fingers through the holes) to explain the activity. Be sure the puppets do the talking.

WRITE YOUR PLAY

Finish each of the finger puppets.
Write a play for your characters.
Then cut out the puppets and present your play.

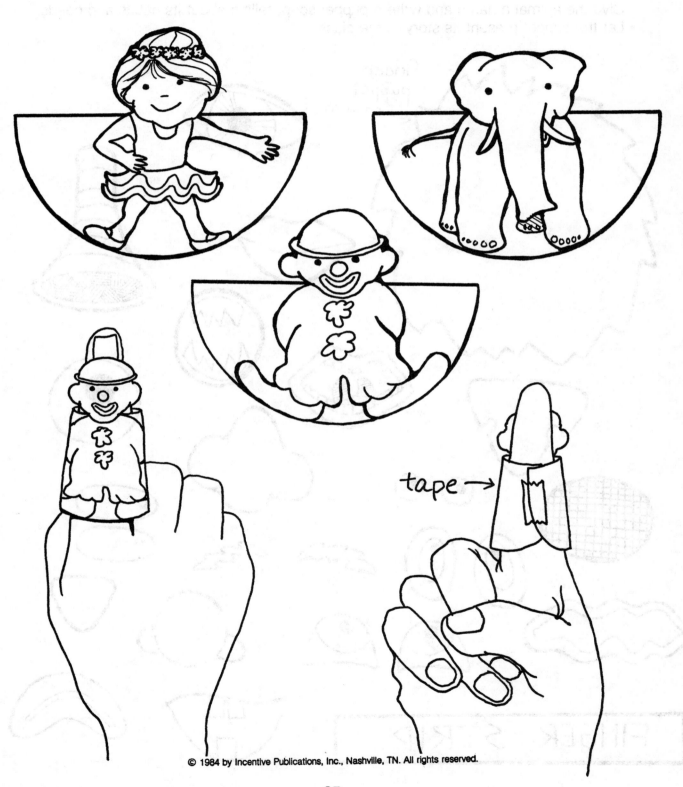

tape →

A STRANGE ANIMAL
WITH A TALE TO TELL

Select some of the parts below to put together and make a funny, one-of-a-kind animal puppet. Color the parts, cut them out and glue them on the finger puppet form. Then cut around the figure and the finger strip to complete the puppet.

Give the animal a name and write a puppet script telling about its habits and needs. Let the puppet present its story to the class.

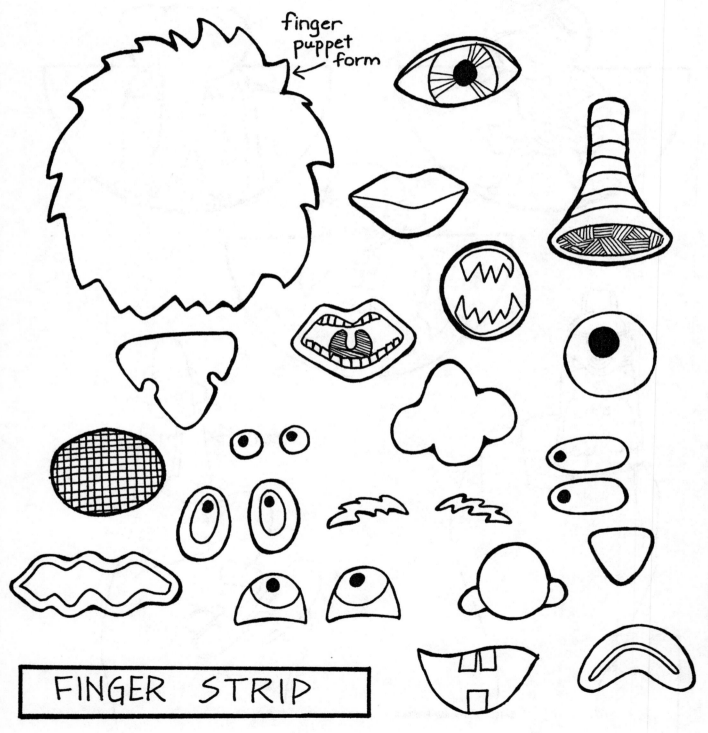

finger
puppet
form

FINGER STRIP

PUPPET PASTE UP

Select any of the items below to complete a paper bag puppet. Color the items, cut them out and paste them on a bag to make your puppet. Give the puppet a name and write a play for it.

Note
Ask a friend to use the leftovers to make a companion for your puppet. Then both of you write a play for the 2 puppets.

PUPPET MAKER'S BOOKSHELF

To get a head start on making and using puppets, you need lots of good books to get ideas from. Begin now to fill this bookshelf with titles of fairy and folk tales, rhymes, songs, plays and games to help you with your puppets and plays.

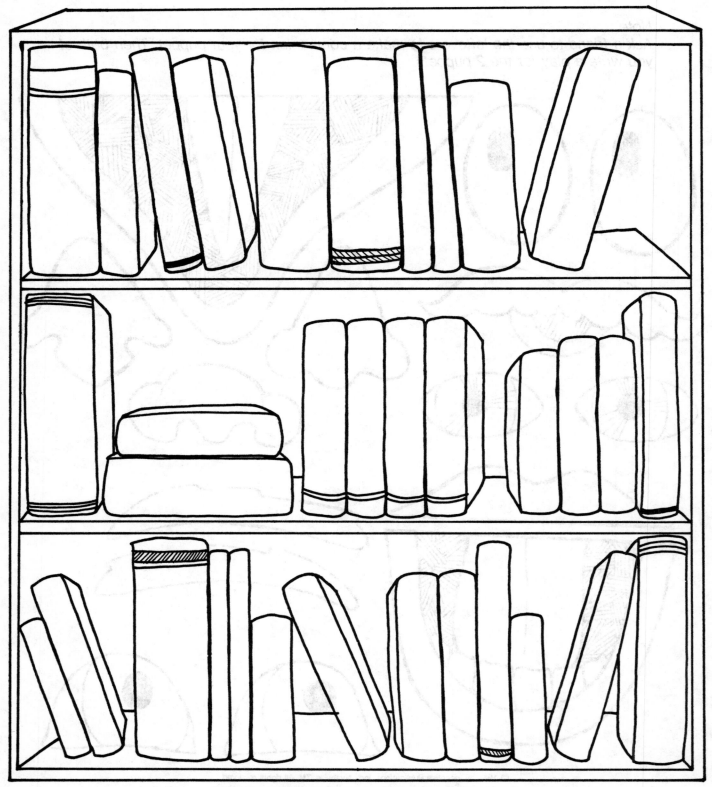

SELECTED LISTING
OF KIDS' STUFF BOOKS
To help puppet makers make, use and enjoy hundreds of other creative learning projects

I Can Make a Rainbow by Marjorie Frank
Rainbow-colored pages with delightful illustrations and easy-to-read step-by-step instructions to stretch imaginations and provide hours of creative arts and crafts experiences.

Puddles & Wings & Grapevine Swings by Imogene Forte and Marjorie Frank
Brightly colored pages with directions for indoor or outdoor projects and adventures. Includes crafts for all seasons; games and activities for backyard or the wide open spaces; things to grow; things to do with sticks, stones, sand and mud; weather and ecology experiments.

Let Loose on Mother Goose by Terry Graham
Twenty-one favorite nursery rhymes are used to teach math, science, art, music, life skills and language development.

Teacher's Gold Mine by Dorothy Michener and Beverly Muschlitz
A treasury of reproducible game boards, skills-based activity pages, pin-ups, self-correcting devices and patterns, plus ideas for easily made bulletin boards and other instructional aids.

Rainy Day—Magic for Wonderful Wet Weather by Imogene Forte
This book provides children with outdoor activites to help them get in touch with nature, indoor experiments to while away the hours and opportunities for finding answers to rainy day questions.

The Real Happily Ever After Book
A marvelous introduction to the world of fantasy! Twenty-one favorite fairy tales written in dialogue form, ready to use with large or small groups. The reproducible masks, puppets, stand-ups, cut and paste projects plus much more can be used in a variety of ways.

Holidays—Special Ways To Celebrate Special Days by Imogene Forte
This book captures the festive spirit associated with holidays the world over with a variety of creative projects and activities to enhance the joy of celebration and to build lasting memories.

Arts and Crafts—From Things Around the House by Imogene Forte
This book shows children that a variety of attractive and useful creations can be made from simple materials readily available in the form of household throwaways. Each activity invites creativity and allows children to discover the thrill and reward of accomplishment.

Patterns, Projects and Plans To Perk Up Early Learning Programs
by Imogene Forte
Over 175 reproducible patterns, each backed with teaching ideas; strategies; art, drama, music, language and math activities to develop basic skills. Additional lesson plans, skills overviews, letters to parents, annotated bibliographies, plus games, mazes and recipes make this a "must-have" book for every teacher of young children!

Of Rhinoceros Wings & More Usual Things by Imogene Forte and Joy MacKenzie
A creative arts book for the young child which contributes to the development of a sound foundation necessary for school readiness. Every page has been planned to provide activities which will enhance the child's self-concept and interest in learning.

INDEX